c

St. Helens Libraries

Please return / renew this item by the last date shown.
Books may be renewed by phone and Internet.

Telephone - (01744) 676954 or 677822
Email - centrallibrary@sthelens.gov.uk
Online - sthelens.gov.uk/librarycatalogue
Twitter - twitter.com/STHLibraries

D0582086

GOVERNMENT & DEMOCRACY

by

Charlie Ogden

©2017
Book Life
King's Lynn
Norfolk PE30 4LS

ISBN: 978-1-78637-116-4

Written by:
Charlie Ogden

Edited by:
Grace Jones

Designed by:
Drue Rintoul

Photocredits
Abbreviations: l-left, r-right, b-bottom, t-top, c-centre, m-middle.

Front Cover t – Samot. Front Cover b – Alessia Pierdomenico. 2 – James Jones Jr. 4 – Sobolev_Igor. 5 – MyImages – Micha. 6 – Georgios Kollidas. 7 – yurchello108. 8 – Phil MacD Photography. 9t – Alexey Stiop. 9b – Pim Leijen. 10 – Drop of Light. 11 – Ilaszlo. 12 – David Fowler. 13t – alice-photo. 13bl – Terry Moore, via Wikimedia Commons. 13br – By U.S. Department of State [Public domain], via Wikimedia Commons. 14t – Everett Collection. 14bl – holbox. 14bm – Andrea Izzotti. 14br – Erik Cox Photography. 15 – Steve Heap. 16 – leungchopan. 17 – Viktoria Gaman. 18 – s_jakkarin. 19 – Jan Wellmann. 20 – bikeriderlondon. 21bl – David Fowler. 21br – Christopher Elwell. 22 – Featureflash Photo Agency. 23 – Everett Historical. 24 – diplomedia. 25 – Slavko Sereda. 26 – Rich Lynch. 27 – milosk50. 29 – knyazevfoto.ru.
Images are courtesy of Shutterstock.com, unless stated otherwise. With thanks to Getty Images, Thinkstock Photo and iStockphoto.

CONTENTS

Words in **bold** can be found in the glossary on page 31.

WHAT IS A GOVERNMENT?

A government is a group of people put in place by a **society**. It provides rules, **authority** and order for the people in that society. Today, every country in the world has a government. For many countries this is a good thing, as a government is able to organise the people and **resources** in a country in the way that is best for its **citizens**. However, while governments are supposed to do all they can to help the people in their countries, some governments are more effective at doing this than others.

WE CALL DEBATES AND QUESTIONS ABOUT HOW GOVERNMENTS SHOULD WORK 'POLITICS'.

The Grand Kremlin Palace in Moscow, Russia. It is home to the president of the Russian government.

In order for the people in a government to be able to help and protect the citizens in their country, they need to be able to do a lot of things. They need to have the power to stop people from doing harmful things, the ability to help people who are in trouble and the resources to build **facilities** for their community, amongst many other things.

For a government to achieve all of this, it needs a lot of money. One way that governments often raise this money is through tax. Governments use the money that they raise through taxes to buy large and often expensive buildings for the people in their countries to use, such as schools and hospitals. The Queen Elizabeth Hospital in Birmingham, England cost over 500 million pounds to build!

This is what police officers look like in India.

WHAT IS TAX?

Tax is the money that the people in a country pay to their government so that the government can do things like pay for police officers, help people who are disabled and build schools, roads and hospitals.

WHY IS A GOVERNMENT IMPORTANT?

Sometimes people find it difficult to understand why having a government is important. In these situations, **philosopher** Thomas Hobbes said that people should think about what life would be like if there had never been a government. If there was no government, people would be more likely to commit crimes, such as coming into your home and taking whatever they wanted, because there would be no laws or police officers to stop them. Governments help to provide protection and safety to the people that they govern; they try to make it so that a **community** of people can live and work together peacefully.

Thomas Hobbes

MONEY

Money is very important for communities all around the world, as it allows people to buy things that they don't already have. Without governments, however, it is unlikely that our system of money would work as well as it does. This is because governments are the ones who are able to organise a country's citizens into agreeing that the little pieces of paper and metal, which we call money, actually mean something.

If you think about it, money doesn't actually have any value itself; you can't eat it as food or make clothes out of it. Money only has value because everyone agrees that it has value. For example, a butcher knows that the money he makes selling bacon can be used to buy anything else he wants. Without a government, people might not be certain that the money that they have could be used to buy other things.

THE OLDEST COIN EVER FOUND WAS DISCOVERED IN TURKEY AND IS OVER 2,500 YEARS OLD.

7

DISASTERS

Natural disasters, such as floods and earthquakes, may leave people homeless, without food or water and in a great amount of danger. When this happens, governments are some of the only people who can provide **aid** on a large scale, because they have the resources and money to do so. Governments will often have emergency money that is only allowed to be spent in these types of situation. For example, during floods governments may send in boats to the people who are in danger from the flood waters, parachute-in food supplies from aeroplanes and work to reduce the level of the flood waters – all at the same time! If the disaster is particularly bad, a government can also organise fund-raising schemes or ask the governments of other countries for additional help.

Flooding in 2015 in York, England. The British Army was sent in by the UK government to provide aid.

LAWS

One of the most important things that a government can do for a country is make its laws. These are rules that everyone in a country must follow. A country's laws are meant to protect the people in that country. People who do not follow the law are committing a crime, which they can be punished for. A person may be sent to prison, have to pay a fine or work within the community for free as part of their punishment.

However, even though it is the government that decides what should become law, often a country's citizens are able to influence the government's decision. Sometimes the opinions of the public, as well as pressure from the media, can push a government to pass a law. This is because governments know that they should try to listen to public opinion as they have been chosen to represent the people of that country.

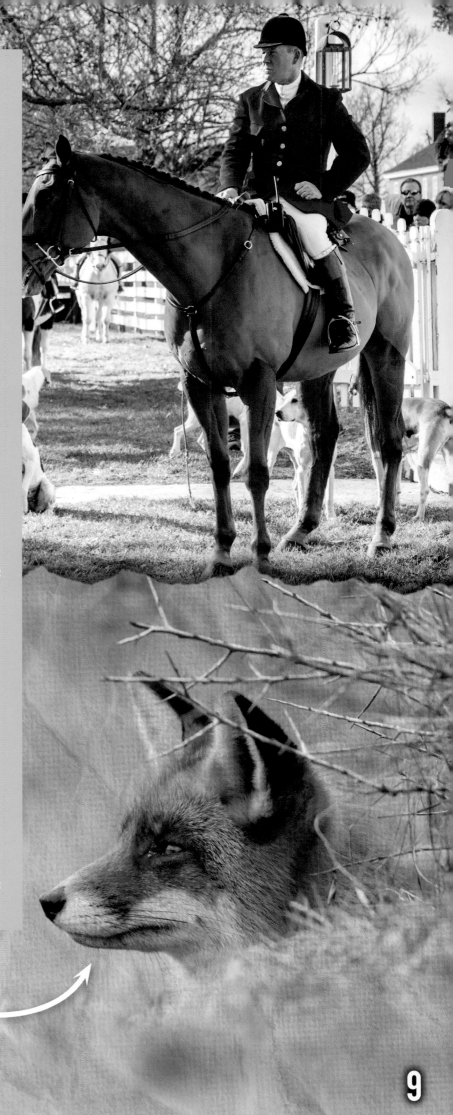

Fox hunting was banned in the UK in 2004 due to pressure from the public and the media.

Here, all the members of the US government are listening to a speech by the president of Ukraine.

The Ukrainian flag.

Governments are often the best at making new laws that are fair for everyone. While some laws are easy to make because almost everyone agrees with them, sometimes laws can involve a lot of complicated factors, such as the laws that determine how much tax different people should pay. Governments are best at deciding what these laws should be because they have the money, information and manpower that is needed to work out what would be best for everyone.

Governments are also good at making laws because they are made up of lots of different people. If just one person made all the laws, they could make laws that only help them. As governments are made up of lots of people who have to agree on what is best, individual people can't make laws that only benefit them.

LAWS AROUND THE WORLD

A government can usually only make laws for its own country. This means that different countries around the world sometimes have very different laws. In the UK, there are laws that state that **equality** must exist between all people. However, not all governments have such laws. In fact, some governments around the world have made laws that stop women from doing things that men are still allowed to do.

One country that has many laws that **prohibit** women from doing certain things is Saudi Arabia. In Saudi Arabia, there are laws that state that women can't drive cars, wear make-up or go outside without having a male with them. Lots of governments around the world – like the UK government – believe that this is wrong. This is because they believe that men and women are equal and should have access to the same rights and opportunities.

Saudi Arabia is the only country in the world that prohibits women from driving.

11

PRIME MINISTERS AND PRESIDENTS

Governments are organised in many different ways, some of which are very complicated. However, most governments will have a single person who is considered to be the head of that government. This person is usually called a prime minister or president.

This is Margaret Thatcher, who was prime minister of the UK from 1979 to 1990.

UK GOVERNMENT

In the UK, the head of the government is called the prime minister. The two most important parts of the UK government are the prime minister and the Cabinet. The Cabinet is made up of 21 senior members of the government who are chosen by the prime minister. Every week the members of the Cabinet and the prime minister come together to discuss the most important issues that the government are facing at that particular time. It is the job of the UK government to develop new **policies**, make sure that all policies are being followed and to put forward suggestions for new laws.

PARLIAMENT

Even though it is the government that suggests new laws in the UK, it cannot **officially** make a new law until Parliament has agreed to it. Parliament is a group of over one thousand people who are responsible for debating the suggestions of the government and approving, amending or voting against new laws that the government may want to create. This means that Parliament doesn't suggest new ways to run the country, instead it can only accept, amend or reject the ideas put forward by the government.

This is the Palace of Westminster, the building where the UK Parliament meets. Parliament has two main parts – the House of Lords and the House of Commons.

PARLIAMENT

HOUSE OF LORDS

Made up of people chosen by the prime minister or an independent organisation. There are also **hereditary** members. There are around 820 members of the House of Lords and the number keeps rising every year!

HOUSE OF COMMONS

Made up of Members of Parliament (MPs) who have been **elected** by the public. There are 650 members of the House of Commons.

US GOVERNMENT

In the US, the head of the government is called the president. However, the president is only one part of the US government. When the United States of America first became a country, a document was written that explained how the government should be set up and how the country should be run. This document is called the United States Constitution and it explains that the US government should have three parts so that no individual person or group can ever have too much power.

Barack Obama, the 44th President of the United States.

US GOVERNMENT

CONGRESS	THE PRESIDENT	THE SUPREME COURT
NUMBER OF PEOPLE:	NUMBER OF PEOPLE:	NUMBER OF PEOPLE:
535	1	9

CONGRESS

The role of Congress in the US government is very similar to that of the House of Commons in the UK government. They are a group of people who are responsible for suggesting, amending and deciding new laws and policies for the country.

THE PRESIDENT

The president is the most important person in the US government. The president has to agree that the new laws and policies suggested by Congress are going to benefit the American people. It is the president's job to work out the most effective way to put them into action.

THE SUPREME COURT

The job of the Supreme Court is to make sure that none of the new laws suggested by Congress go against what is said in the US Constitution. The Supreme Court also decides what certain laws actually mean in cases where it is uncertain whether a law has been broken or not.

The United States Supreme Court building.

GOVERNMENTS AROUND THE WORLD

JAPAN

Japan formed a new government in 1947, after the **Second World War**, and wrote a **constitution** that explained how the new government should run the country. There is a specific part of the Japanese Constitution that is unlike the constitution of any other government in the world – it prohibits Japan from ever going to war. Japan has not fought a war against another country since the

Second World War and if it follows its own constitution, it never will. Japan still has an army, but it cannot use it to attack other countries. Instead, the army has remained in case Japan is attacked by another country and needs to defend itself.

The Japanese flag.

Japan

Tokyo, the capital city of Japan.

NORTH KOREA

The government of North Korea is one of the most well-known governments in the world. North Korea became a country in 1948 and when it did a man called Kim Il-sung was made the president. Since then, the North Korean government has become a dictatorship where rule over the country has passed straight from father to son without a democratic election.

DICTATORSHIP

A dictatorship is a form of government where one person, or sometimes a small group of people, makes all of the decisions for a country.

Pyongyang, the capital city of North Korea.

North Korea

The North Korean flag.

For over 60 years, North Korea has been a dictatorship. Because of this, decisions have been made that only seem to benefit the government rather than the public. The North Korean dictator, Kim Jong-un, and many people who are close to him seem to live expensive lifestyles in big houses, whereas much of the North Korean population struggles to find enough food to survive. However, it is difficult to be exactly sure what is going on in North Korea as it is one of the most secretive countries in the world and the government only lets very few people enter the country.

BHUTAN

Bhutan is a very small country in Asia. However, in 1972, Bhutan introduced a policy that would change the way that **politicians** around the world thought about what made a successful government. The King of Bhutan, known as Dragon King Jigme Singye Wangchuck, declared that the happiness of the people in Bhutan should be used to measure how well the country's government was doing. In Bhutan, Gross National Happiness is the most important factor in measuring the government's success or failure.

The Bhutanese flag.

The United Nations (UN) flag. The UN is an important organisation that works with governments all over the world. They have, along with Bhutan, made happiness one of their main considerations when deciding how successful a government is.

Bhutan

Thimphu, the capital city of Bhutan.

SOMALIA

Somalia was once a very powerful country, however in recent years it has had one of the most unstable governments in the world. In 1991, a **civil war** broke out in Somalia and the Somali government was removed from power by some of the Somali public. A new government could not be formed in Somalia for many years as the civil war and a severe **drought** used much of the country's resources, making it very difficult for any group of people to create change in the country. This left Somalia in a state of **anarchy**.

In 2000, a Somali government was established for the first time in nearly ten years. However, this new government was only ever in control of a very small amount of Somalia, leaving most of Somalia's population to have to try to survive the civil war without help from a government.

The Somali flag.

Mogadishu, the capital city of Somalia.

Somalia

The Somali parliament finally met in 2012, after 17 attempts to create a new government. By this time, most of the country had spent over 20 years living without a government.

WHAT IS A DEMOCRACY?

Living within a democracy means that the people in a country get to take part in the decisions made by their government – they are able to have a say in how their country is governed. Any kind of government that is influenced by public opinion is called a democracy; however, this doesn't mean that all democracies are the same. In the past, it used to be the case that only men, or even just rich men, could take part in the decisions of a government. Nowadays, lots of countries accept that everyone should have a say in a democracy and usually the only condition is that you have to be above a certain age.

There are two main types of democracy; a direct democracy and a representative democracy. These two types of democracy relate to the ways in which people can take part in the decisions of their governments.

DIRECT AND REPRESENTATIVE DEMOCRACIES

A direct democracy is where the public can vote on every decision made by their government. This is often not a realistic way to run a government, especially in countries with lots of people. Governments in big countries have to make lots of decisions and there often isn't enough time to find out what everyone in the country wants the government to do.

People in representative democracies instead vote on who is in their governments. Every few years, people in representative democracies can vote on who they want to govern their countries – these are called **general elections**. After the votes have been counted and a government has been chosen, the people in that country usually do not get to vote on every law or policy. Instead, their elected representatives do this on behalf of the general public. If the public feel that the government is not representing their interests, they can choose to vote for a different party or politician during the next general election.

The UK government is a representative democracy and usually has a general election every 5 years. The main two **political parties** in the UK are Conservative and Labour.

VOTE FOR CHANGE

Vote Conservative

VOTE Labour

Labour

vote

labour

bour

labour.org.uk

Labour

WHAT ISN'T A DEMOCRACY?

MONARCHY

Another way of governing a country is through a monarchy, which is where just one member of a royal family, called the monarch, rules over a country. While every member of the ruling family in a monarchy will have some power, only the monarch is considered to be the leader of the country. When the monarch dies, another member of the same family takes over, usually their eldest son. In Europe, the person who rules a monarchy is usually called a king or a queen, whereas in Asia they are often called an emperor or an empress.

This is the case in the UK. Queen Elizabeth II is technically the ruler of the UK, but the democratic government makes almost all of the important decisions.

There are very few monarchies left in the world today and many of the monarchies that do still exist don't really count as a monarchy. This is because the king, queen, emperor or empress in these countries do not have much actual power. Instead, these countries often have a government that does most of the actual running of the country.

One of the most famous dictators of all time was Adolf Hitler, who was the German dictator before and during the Second World War.

The leader of a dictatorship, known as a dictator, can gain power in a number of ways. Sometimes they work their way up through a democratic government and then, when they have enough power to do so, they change the government into a dictatorship and put themselves in charge. Other times, civil war may break out in the country. During the civil war, a group of people who want there to be a change in the country's government will force the government out of power and will put their own dictator in charge instead.

WHY IS A DEMOCRACY IMPORTANT?

Democratic governments have been seen to time and time again produce two outcomes in particular: the freedom of their people and a **stable government**. Democracy is so important because it often leads to these two things.

Some countries that aren't considered to be democratic don't give their citizens the freedom to choose their own religion. This is the case in Saudi Arabia, where every citizen must be Muslim by law.

Most people want the freedom to choose what religion they follow, where they live and who they marry. Most democracies encourage freedom as they listen to and act upon the views and beliefs of the people that they govern. For something to become law in a democratic government, a majority of people have to agree that it should be a law. However, extreme views about marriage, religion and where people should live aren't often held by a majority of people. This stops extreme views from being made into laws in democratic governments, meaning that citizens in democratic countries often have their freedom.

Democratic countries, if run properly, often have the support of many of their citizens. This is because they will be run by publicly elected politicians and so they usually try to represent the public's interests. This greatly reduces the chance of civil war in democratic countries as people are not likely to attack a government with which they agree.

Countries that are run by a dictator, on the other hand, are more likely to break out into civil war. Dictators can do anything they want with their countries and are almost always unelected. This can lead to some people starting a civil war in order to remove the dictator.

In 2011, a civil war broke out in Libya in order to overthrow the dictator Muammar Gaddafi.

DEMOCRACY IN HISTORY

Many people believe that the principles of democracy were first founded over 2,500 years ago in the ancient city of Athens. Athens is now the capital city of Greece, however at that point in time it was an independent city that acted much like a country does today.

This is the Parthenon, a temple dedicated to the Ancient Greek goddess Athena. It was built during the time that Athens was a democracy, roughly 2,500 years ago.

Until this point in history, nearly all countries were controlled by a monarch or a dictator and so a lot of people in Athens at the time were interested and excited by the new idea of democracy. However, there was one person in particular who did not like the idea of Athens being a democracy – Plato. Plato was a famous philosopher who lived thousands of years ago in Athens and he thought that democracy was a bad idea because most people are not capable of running a country. He thought that the people of Athens would only make poor decisions about how to run the city and that a better idea would be to let only the most intelligent people in Athens have a say in how the city was run.

Athens had a direct democracy, so the public could vote on every decision made by the government in Athens. However, in many ways the democracy in Athens wasn't a very good democracy.

The main way in which the government in Athens failed to be a good democracy was that it didn't allow everyone to vote. Only the richer men in the community could vote – poor men, women and slaves had no say in what the government did. However, this is not very unusual for the time. In the UK, women were not given the same right to vote as men until 1928. This shows that even though the democratic government of Athens wasn't perfect, it was still very ahead of its time.

The Acropolis of Athens.

Athens was conquered around 2,400 years ago and became a monarchy under the rule of King Philip II of Macedonia. Athens had a democrctic government for less than 200 years and only returned to a democratic system some 2,000 years later.

DEMOCRACY IN THE WORLD

Sometimes it can be very difficult to know whether a country has a democratic government or not. This is because governments are often very large and have a lot of different parts to them. This can sometimes mean that one part of a government works democratically and another part doesn't work democratically.

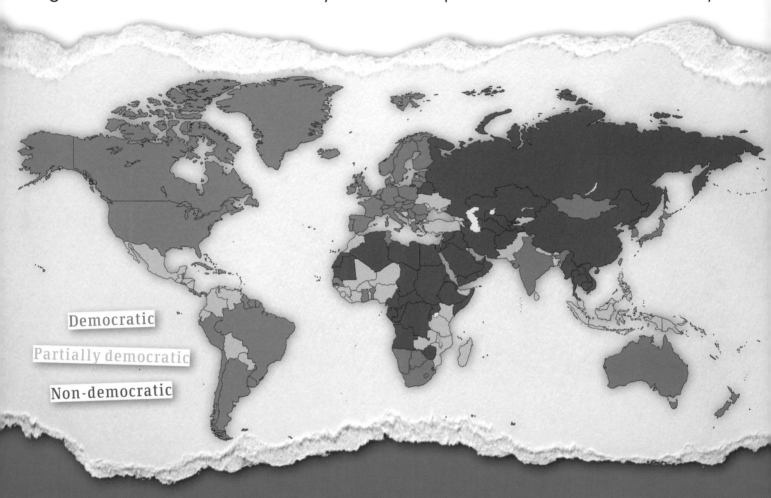

Democratic

Partially democratic

Non-democratic

Lots of studies have been done in order to determine which countries are democratic and which are not. Most countries in Africa and Asia do not have democratic governments but instead are ruled by some sort of dictatorship. Many other countries in Africa and Asia, and some in South America, have governments that have some elements of a democracy and some elements of a dictatorship. This is a good sign – it shows that countries in these areas are beginning to move towards a democratic form of government.

Most democratic governments today exist in western Europe, North America and South America. However, there are strong democratic governments outside of these areas, such as in Australia, Japan, South Africa and India. India is the largest democratic country in the world and collected over 800 million votes in its last general election.

The most democratic countries in the world, according to the Democracy Index, are in northern Europe. Norway, Sweden, Denmark and other countries in the same area of Europe are believed by many to have the most stable and democratic governments in the world.

This is possibly because of the size of these countries. Many of the countries in this area of Europe are very small and have populations of fewer than 10 million people, which makes it a lot easier to maintain a strong democratic government and collect votes from everyone in the country. However, this can't be the only reason that they are democratic, as there are lots of countries that are even smaller than these that do not have democratic governments.

A man in India's capital, New Delhi.

ACTIVITIES

Be like Thomas Hobbes! In what ways would life change if there were no governments giving rules, order and protection to communities?

How many democratic countries can you think of?
Use the map below to help you!

Democratic

Partially democratic

Non-democratic

GLOSSARY

aid	help given to people in a disaster by a government or charity
anarchy	a disordered community caused by the lack of an authority or government
authority	the power to give orders or make decisions
citizens	legally recognised members of a country
civil war	a war between citizens of the same country
community	a group of people who live and work in the same area
constitution	a collection of rules that state how a government should work
drought	a long period of very little rainfall, which leads to a lack of water
elected	voted for by the public
equality	the state of being equal, especially in rights, status and opportunity
facilities	buildings or pieces of equipment provided for a specific purpose
general elections	where the main parties in governments are voted for by the public
hereditary	passed down from a parent to a child
officially	with the authority of the government
philosopher	a person who studies the nature of knowledge, reality and existence
policies	courses of action adopted by organisations or governments
political parties	organised groups of people who have similar ideas about government
politicians	people who are professionally involved in the government and politics
prohibit	formally forbidden by a law or rule
resources	supplies of money, materials or people
Second World War	a major war fought between 1939 and 1945
society	a large collection of people made up of many communities
stable government	a government that is resistant to sudden change or collapse

INDEX